The Butterfly Spreads its Wings

By Anna Delves

Author of 'From Chrysalis to Butterfly'

authorHOUSE®

AuthorHouse™ UK Ltd.
500 Avebury Boulevard
Central Milton Keynes, MK9 2BE
www.authorhouse.co.uk
Phone: 08001974150

First published by AuthorHouse   04/25/2011

ISBN: 978-1-4567-7537-7 (sc)
ISBN: 978-1-4567-7538-4 (e)

To lose a son is devastating, but to receive such deep revelations from him from the 'other' side was mind blowing.

He and I invite you to learn and grow as you read this book.

Contents

Foreword

.....................In the beginning was light, and the light was in darkness, and the darkness comprehended it not..................

All that existed was 'light' or nothingness. And yet, because of the light, darkness existed, darkness being the opposite of light and being the word used here to depict 'that which the light didn't know'. And so the two grew together, in equal measure...........

So, right from the beginning, light grew through the universe from the source, feeling its way along the journey, spreading gently through the universal system, knowing its contact with the source and feeling the constant need to 'push forward' into the unknown.

It met planets on its way and integrated with their masses, bringing light into their systems in various ways. Each planet brought its own 'teaching' allowing the light more knowledge of itself as it 'experienced' each time.

The following writings are gifted by my beloved eldest son, Dom, who left this life on July 2nd 2008. I gift these revelations to you, in order that you may understand as much as you can, thus helping to release your own unique 'light' back onto our planet.

Introduction

The mystery of creation has been a source of interest to man from the earliest ages. But I was one of the people who never really delved far into these mysteries, always being more concerned with the here and now. Therefore it was with the greatest surprise that I began to receive revelations in the early part of 2009 which unveiled a simple yet completely understandable account of how this planet has evolved.

The revelations have mostly been transmitted to me by my son. As he lay dying I bravely asked the universe if I could learn and grow as much as possible from the experience. Little did I know the enormity of the story that was about to unfold! However, I was told, shortly after his death, that I would receive a gift, but I had no idea what it would be. When the revelations started to come I knew *they* were the gift and I was bowled over that I should be entrusted with such deep and amazing knowledge.

Since that time I have been sharing what I can of this knowledge with the appropriate people, learning at the same time, how to communicate it, when to communicate it and which parts to communicate. It has been completely exhausting for me to continually repeat and explain these revelations and it has taken several hearings before my listeners have actually grasped enough of what I have been trying to convey, to allow them to truly benefit. This book is my attempt to put everything into words.

It is my intention to share with you all as much as I can. Most has been received in big chunks, but some came in little pieces and some whilst listening to the responses of my audiences on various different occasions. **Ask to learn all that you can as you read** and you will benefit for your own and the planet's highest good.

Chapter One

The first set of revelations

I was walking my dogs one afternoon, something I do every day, when I suddenly became aware that my deceased son, Dom, was walking beside me. This was not too unusual an event, but when it happens I always feel overjoyed and so thankful that I can feel him there. As we walked along on that particular day, in calm companionship, I suddenly felt him move all around me. It felt as if his energy was encompassing my whole body and giving me a huge hug. I was delighted!

As we progressed along the woodland path I felt as if spirit and incarnated soul had become one. It felt as if my son and I were one. It was fabulous. I gradually became aware that my consciousness was no longer solely confined to my body but that it was also in quite a big area outside my body. I therefore felt as if I was walking amongst and through the trees that surrounded me and that I was far, far bigger than my physical self. I began to communicate with the trees and the other parts of nature I was passing. I heard the trees telling me their history; how they communicated with each other, how they touched each other and how they were aware of each other in differing ways. I passed one tree valiantly holding up another tree and I said to it,

"Why are you doing this? Your friend has nearly died and needs to fall. You are wasting your energy and also preventing your friend from moving on into spirit"

I felt the tree's shocked surprise and I left it to ponder!

I started to communicate telepathically with my dogs and achieved getting one of them to come and stand at my feet without using my voice. She had previously been running around the wood like a mad thing! I was so excited! I felt the trappings of my earthly body had been hugely removed. I was ecstatic. This is what I had wanted for so long but had always thought I would have to wait until I died before it could be achieved!

After a while the woodland path started to go up a hill and as I trudged slowly upwards with my consciousness still expanding, I started to think about energy and where it came from. What exactly was taking my body up the hill? What was gravity? What *was* energy? What was propelling my body forwards?

The next moment I became aware of my consciousness sliding down a huge dark tube and the tube was going *within*. It was very weird. Then my slide came to a stop and I knew I was at the centre of the earth. I was light and everything around me was extremely black. I heard a deep booming voice, not my son's, say,

"What you are about to learn now relates to this planet and this planet only"

I thought a surprised, "ok" and wondered what was going to happen next.

From my new perspective at the very core of the earth I felt the emotion that came from the light as it wriggled and squirmed around in itself in its enforced prison. I felt the 'trap' that the light was in and I knew its frustration as it sought to find out what had happened to it and where it was. It seemed as if the emotion was in some sort of fight with itself. It felt dark and swirly and I knew it was searching for its own 'freedom'. As it fought it started to move and as it moved it started to expand. I didn't know it at the time but I know now that this momentous occasion was the first moment on *this* planet that we (light) felt the separation from source. It was an illusion of course. We were the source......... But the entrapment in the apparent dark space caused the light to feel a type of separation and as it expanded further and further into the mass that was the earth, the separation 'seemed' more and more real.

I felt this process go on for a while and then felt quite awed as I started to see the strata of the earth forming as the emotional upheaval pushed and shoved in various different directions. I saw the emotions criss-crossing each other in their attempt to know who they were and I felt the emotion from the core getting larger and larger as the struggle continued. There were different earth patterns forming everywhere. Some of the light/emotion swirled in circles around the core, some seemed to shoot outwards towards the earth's crust in a straightish line, and some wriggled its way about, weaving in and around whatever it encountered. There was no set pattern. It was a changing vibrant energy on the move.

Inch by inch, the light shifted outwards from the core.

When the light/emotion grew large enough to reach the earth's crust I felt a change as the resistance it encountered altered. There was a long moment of calm, as if the whole planet was drawing in its breath and then eruptions began all over the planet's surface. The trapped emotion from within was hastening to the freedom of what it thought was the light that it sensed was possibly without. I experienced massive volcanoes as the emotion shot out from what had felt like a prison. I felt earthquakes taking place both under water and above ground, as the bottled emotion from the core exploded onto the earth's surface in varying formats. I experienced an incredible exploding of the mass that we call earth.

I remained connected to this explosive environment for quite a while, sensing the rush, sensing the light's search for freedom and feeling the enormity of the experience as I did so.

I realised that the emotions that were erupting all over the planet had each taken their own, completely unique, routes to the surface. All these routes that were criss-crossing each other and erupting in millions of different ways were us, remembering the different routes that we (emotion/light) had taken from the earth's core. I realised immediately why we have all known each other over and over again and that it started from the moment that the light started to move. Our 'knowing' of each other began at the very beginning of it all.

Gradually, I suppose over millions of earth years, I felt the planet begin to calm. The eruptions became less severe and the earth's crust showed signs of lessening anger.............

At this point my son fast forwarded my consciousness to a much calmer phase when I felt the emotion trying to poke out from the earth's crust. I can only describe it as a distinct prickly sensation that I felt all over the planet's surface.

The first 'pokers' came out as grasses, tiny shoots that lasted for a millionth of a second and then disappeared. This was the beginnings of what we now call the 'life cycle'. The emotion *wanted* to experience the air, light and the water and above all the freedom that it sensed was there and it kept on poking. Gradually grass learnt to exist longer and longer. Life cycles changed constantly as it did so. It spent time incarnate and it spent time in spirit. When it was in spirit it hugged the earth surface closely, not wanting to lose the opportunity of reincarnating when it could. I lived the process closely and knew that the grasses all over the planet were emerging in many different guises, depending on the route they had taken from the source and depending on the climate they hit outside. I felt a process of the whole of the emotion from the light straining to exist beyond the earth's surface and gradually forming as different varieties of our 'nature'.

My son then once again fast forwarded the 'slide' show and showed me a tree. This was at the time when the tree was the king of creation. Trees had gradually learnt to outlive the grass's short life cycle and survive for a number of years. He showed me the tree communicating with its near neighbours by brushing their branches together as the wind blew. He showed me the baby trees that were growing up quietly at their parent's base.

But as emotion/light from the centre of the earth kept on pushing for knowledge/freedom, there came a moment when I felt the tree looking out over the horizon and sensing other trees at a distance. These were trees that it had no communication with. They were too far away. But it *wanted* communication. I felt such a yearning, such a massive desire to communicate, from the tree that eventually (from this desire) underground creatures started to form. They were tiny, bloodless creatures, worm like, or even maggot like, and silent. I felt them creating themselves within the trunk of the tree and then emerging from the base of the tree and starting to make their way towards the other trees.

As they felt the 'push' to make the journey from one tree to another, (or from one place to another) they mistakenly felt they were undergoing a much greater 'separation' from the light/source. Those first maggots did not survive for very long. A sort of panic ensued! They felt too separated from source to make the journey. The trees felt connected because they were connected to the ground. The worms/ maggots felt an immense sense of disconnection as they tried to leave the tree, moving in a way that appeared to them to be 'alone'. So the grasses on the path between the trees called to the worms/maggots, to absorb their nutrients.

"Eat me. Feed off me! Absorb me," they called, seeing it as a way for the journeyers to stay connected to the source and therefore have the energy/ability to survive the apparent 'disconnected' distance. Thus the first form of eating began; the first form of this type of dependence upon each other and the first part of the illusion that we, in animal or human form, need to eat/absorb each other to survive.

I was then taken through a fairly quick process, enabling me to experience the gradual formation of all underground animals, then over ground/underground animals and finally over ground animals, developing after thousands, possibly millions of years into humans. As they developed the eating process developed, all in the name of survival. They all believed that by sustaining one another in this way, the unrooted would somehow remain fed by the rooted. And once this idea allowed for the survival of the unrooted, it grew unhindered amongst all detached creation, in order that they might survive. So larger animals began to eat smaller animals and humans began to eat them all.

For a fleeting second at this point, the rolling ball of evolution that I was experiencing went on into the future and I became aware that the probability of a 'flying' future was more than likely.

At about this moment I semi came out of the very deep trance state that I had been in and became aware of my surroundings a little more. Glancing downwards I saw that I was walking up a small, grassy track. The sun was out and while I enjoyed its warmth on my back I noticed the clear, blue sky above. I felt the soft grass beneath my feet and started to apologise to it that I was walking on it and hurting it. This was not the first time in my life that this thought had crossed my mind, for I have often wondered if we hurt the grass when we walk on it, but realised we couldn't avoid it, so dismissed the thought again.

However, as I thought the thought this time, the sudden realisation came that I had *been* the grass that I was walking on; that I had *been* the animals that have eaten the grass, and I had *been* the grass that the animals have eaten. I've been the human that has eaten the animals. I've been the human that the animals have eaten. I felt the grass communicating that it was proud to allow me to walk on it because I was a part of the current, most evolved species of creation. The grass wanted to support me as I walked my path, because what I discovered, I discovered for it too. And I felt the support system throughout the whole of creation as I had never felt it before, and also the complete unity between the whole of incarnated existence.

Stepping out further along my track I started to realise consciously, the enormity and clarity of the revelations I had just received. I marvelled at the whole thing and whilst still feeling somewhat overwhelmed I experienced deep, deep gratitude to Dom for giving me such amazing awareness.

The track I was following came out onto a road, which I crossed and then took the path which led across some fields towards my home. As I crossed the hedged boundary onto my own farmland I found myself slipping back into a trance state again. I felt the universe communicating to me that the farm was now subject to an advanced set of rules and regulations! I was given to understand that the farm had now come 'consciously' under the direct control of the universe. This meant that it would be a completely safe place for anyone or anything to exist, providing we or it 'towed the line'. For example, if the squirrels ate all the bark off the trees and killed them, they might well find that they themselves would later be run over or shot. If they respected the trees they would find that the trees and the farm would house them perfectly safely. Another example was myself or any other human on the property. As long as I continued to work for the highest good of all creation, I would be nourished and looked after and kept safe on the farm. If I transgressed, I would receive the punishment due. If the deer ate things that they were not supposed to eat, they might find themselves in trouble but if they kept to the places they were entitled to graze they would be quite safe.

These rules would apply to anyone or anything on the farm, regardless of their status. I also knew that I would have nothing whatsoever to do with the implementing of these rules; it would all be controlled by the great universal law. I felt quite over awed by these huge revelations.

As I walked on, I became aware of a strong, white light coming from the centre of the earth, from the source of all that is, quietly enveloping the whole farm. I felt it was pure, powerful and healing, and of other qualities way beyond my comprehension. I continued my homeward journey in a state of wonder.

What had happened today?

Just what had happened today?

As if to confirm these revelations, I was in my yard a few days later when I saw a barn owl sitting on a low branch of an apple tree. This was a very unusual sight for the middle of the day so I stopped and stared at it, feeling very privileged to have such a good view of it. It sat on the branch so still that I half thought it was a wooden owl. However, a minute or so later it flew off and sat in a nearby cherry tree. I walked towards it as the cherry tree stood right on the path on which I wanted to go. I stopped about three feet away from the branch it was sitting on and stared up at it. It was not much more than eighteen inches above my head. Again I felt it was such a privilege. Then eventually I thought,

"Well, I must go up this path and feed my hens."

I stepped forward, fully believing that the owl would take off as soon as I moved. It did nothing of the sort! It turned its head and watched me walk right under it. I stared up at it and it stared down at me and clearly told me with its huge round trusting eyes that it knew it was safe.

It took me many, many weeks to stop talking about this wonderful owl incident, because nothing like this had ever happened to me before and it really did confirm that everything I had experienced was true.

Over the next few weeks I pondered over the enormity of what I had been shown. My understanding of all the revelations expanded as I tried to repeat them to a few people and they were all equally thrilled by the simplicity of all that had happened.

Not long afterwards, two people I had met only a couple of times before went for a walk around the perimeter of the farm. One of them rang me up and told me of this and asked why the fields on the far side of my boundary had such a horrible energy. I was amazed and said there had *never* been a horrible energy there, it had always been wonderful. She was adamant and said,

"No, it was strongly apparent".

Both she and her friend had felt this unhappy energy on the other side of my boundary but when they looked across at my farm they had sensed an incredibly pure energy emanating from it. The distinction was extraordinary to them. She asked what I had done!

In an instant I pictured the scene where I had been walking across my fields on the day of the revelations and I remembered feeling the universe tell me about the powerful white light. I remembered that I had pictured the white light spreading to the very edge of all my boundaries and rising upwards to the sky. Then I suddenly felt absolutely awful. I realised I had pictured the white light up to the boundaries of my farm and remaining within the boundaries. Of course the surrounding land was angry. I had not seen the white light spreading over the boundaries at will, going wherever it was invited to go.

I tried to explain this to the caller, whilst desperately trying to put the situation right with the universe. I started picturing the light spreading everywhere like mad, worldwide if it wanted to! I felt devastated at what I had done so unwittingly, and yet I felt totally amazed that these two people had seen the light without knowing anything about what I had experienced.

On the next walk that these two good people took around my boundaries they were able to confirm that the energy everywhere was now at peace again. I was so, so grateful to them and so grateful that the universe only allowed this mistake to continue for a few days before causing me to rectify it!

One more point on this particular matter is just to mention that several other people confirmed the powerful energy and white light they could see over the farm from a distance. This all acted as huge confirmation to me that all that had been revealed to me was absolutely correct.

Chapter two

The second set of revelations

Some weeks later I was doing exactly the same walk that I had done on the day when I received the first set of revelations, when I felt Dom surround me again. I was overjoyed and this time accepted the situation a lot more readily, feeling our oneness quickly and with joyous ease.

Straight away I fell into a deep trance state and I knew in an instant I was experiencing the 'Adam and Eve' moment described in the bible. He showed me that this was the moment that the evolution of the planet had reached a fifty/fifty situation. Basically, at the precise moment that fifty per cent of our planet was incarnate, (this included, rocks, nature, animals, humans etc.) and fifty per cent was spirit, at this precise moment, there was a split. This was the moment that opposites came into being. There was dark and light, hot and cold, love and fear, etc. In other words it was the moment that the planet became conscious. The opposites gave us knowledge of consciousness. And it all happened very, very quickly.

I was taken first to the 'love' side, which was the side that was still in spirit. The love side remained balanced because it was still in touch with the bigger picture.

I was then taken to the 'fear' side and I experienced the moment that the incarnated became aware of themselves for the very first time. I felt the shock, bewilderment, disbelief, in fact a million different emotions being born. The moment appeared to strip the incarnate beings of their light, spreading what seemed like a real encompassing darkness all over the earth's surface.

Back in the love side again I could feel the shock running through the spiritual world. They were watching the terrible state of confusion that was growing on the incarnate side in a blind panic, saying to each other,

"Whatever shall we do?"

I was taken to the incarnate side once more and I experienced the ongoing confusion. I felt animals and people charging about all over the place. Everything 'appeared' very black. There was screaming from people, erupting of volcanoes, earthquakes shaking the ground, animals bellowing, wind howling, trees falling, torrential rain and storms, thunder and lightening. I cannot begin to describe adequately the combined carnage I felt as I dipped into this unprecedented scene from long ago.

Although....... at some level...... we all know it, intimately.

As I re-experienced this moment of the split, I knew that love was stronger than fear because it could see the bigger picture and for that reason, love was always going to be the more powerful of the two emotions.

The situation in which the planet now found itself (fifty per cent incarnated and fifty per cent in spirit), continued for some time, the spiritual trying to figure out what it could do about it and the physical side running riot. Our planet was experiencing an extremely precarious balancing act and the love side had to control that balance as the physical side was unable to. I knew that this moment was one of the most important moments in the planet's history and is one which we all need to understand, in order to bring the true source light back into our living consciousness.

Emotion had always had the intention of 'knowing' itself and this dodgy situation was *always* going to happen.

The planet rocked on its delicate pivotal point for some hundreds of years. The 'love' side was continually working to find a way to redress the rebalance. At this point I became aware that a type of competitiveness came into being. The only way that rebalancing could begin was from the love side. The fear side was too unaware and out of control, to help. So the love side exerted itself to its highest level and in doing so it became a little competitive, in some way seeing 'who' could achieve the impossible first. This desire, this longing from the love side, to achieve, caused a competitive mountain to emerge, and it *had* to be climbed……………….

By this time I had finished my walk and reached the comforting surroundings of home again. I rushed upstairs to find my bible. Sure enough, as I opened it at Genesis, I read about the dark days that are described there. I had not read those words for decades and when I had previously read them I had not understood them. But on this day I read on and on in awe, understanding only too well, exactly what it was depicting. Very soon I came to the verses on Noah. Here I stopped because I felt myself being strongly drawn away from the biblical pages.

Dropping into a deep trance state once more I became aware that Noah was the very first part of the love side that achieved an incarnation on earth without becoming swamped by fear. Noah successfully brought love/light to our earth in an incarnated state and didn't let the crazy, incarnated world deter him. In other words he was the first saviour of the planet, after the split. He had done what had seemed almost impossible.

I sat back in my chair in disbelief!

Noah!

This man, who to me had only ever been in quite an insignificant Sunday school story that involved taking animals in twos into his arc.

Noah!

As the enormity of who Noah really was slowly sank in I started to realise why the biblical story of God's promise of rainbows, dated back to that time. I had always thought it was odd that God's promise of rainbows should be linked to that event, despite there having been seemingly much bigger events in our history! Now I realised that this *was* one of the biggest event in our history, simply because it took our planet's balance from fifty/fifty to forty nine/fifty one, so to speak. It took us out of immediate danger. I began to see Noah in a very different light than I had ever done before.

Dom took me quickly on to realise that Noah started the process of rebalancing our planet and we have been busy rebalancing ever since. There have been other great teachers helping us at strategic moments, such as Joseph, Mohammed and Jesus. Each have accelerated our progress in their time and spun us faster along our evolutionary path. I realised that our planet is now fast heading towards a much rebalanced state, but this time, as we re-find our balance, we will know it.

I'm not sure when, during these revelations, (which took seven hours to receive) I became aware that the so called Atlantian and Lemurian days were the days preceding the split. I had often had flash backs to those peaceful earth days, that were filled with love and light. Indeed I had deep cravings for that existence. But somewhere amongst what was being shown to me I became aware that the days of Atlantis (for want of a better word) or the peaceful days, ended at the split. The split *had to happen*. It was *always* going to happen. It was a part of a huge experiment by the universe, to see if the emotion could become aware of itself, and survive. There was a chance that it would self-destruct, but of course the love side always had the upper hand because it could see what was coming and help avert the earthly eradication that threatened so dramatically after the split occurred.

For those of you who take on board the fact that we have incarnated over and over again on this planet, first in rock form, then as some kind of vegetation, thirdly as animal and some of us now as human, it could be time to find out who or what you were at the time of the split. During the split we all experienced our very first *conscious* emotions and these emotions have dominated all our subsequent lifetimes. The rebalancing of our planet is currently taking the form of realising these things. The more we realise that all the emotions that are stuck in our various pasts have to be released, including, most importantly, our very first emotions, on which the others all hinge, the closer we humans are to returning to a balance that will bring back the pure love and light that we once knew. When we release our very first emotions, we are free to release everything else that is blocking us and we will be able to serve the planet in a very beautiful way.

Souls experienced the split in every conceivable form. All souls had previously been unconscious light and the shock of the first conscious moments impacted on every soul in a different way.

Examples

Some souls experienced the first 'dark' days for only a few seconds. When the chaos started they were only conscious of a few moments of darkness before they were extinguished/killed. These souls would have returned to source with only a fleeting memory of experiencing this 'darkness'. Upon future reincarnations they have often relived this experience over and over again. At some point after birth something would trigger the 'darkness' again and they would live in confusion, attracting dark forces, without knowing why.

Some souls were literally just making their way towards a new incarnation when the split occurred. Some got catapulted back into the ether and some actually continued the journey and landed very uncomfortably in a physical position they could not comprehend. Some have remained in this stuck state ever since, every time they have reincarnated. These can be very damaged people and each subsequent incarnation has only served to deepen the damage.

I have come across wise old souls who were incarnate at the time of the split and held 'high' positions. Some of them sensed the approach of the split and tried to hold on to the fast fading light. For them the darkness that ensued was a gradual process that they tried to fight off but eventually could not. They are often to be found living very difficult lives now, feeling that somewhere they have let their fellow beings down. Some have felt they can never have the light back because they lost the battle at the time of the split and cannot comprehend that the battle can now be 'won'.

I have tuned into souls who went completely barmy at the time of the split. I particularly remember one who's first conscious moment was of animals seemingly attacking him. (In actual fact they were just rushing towards him in their panic.) As he happened to be holding onto a stick he lashed out at them, killing some of them as they passed. I remember tuning to his astonishment at his first experience of death. Until that moment he had no idea that he could kill. This poor man has reproduced this event in subsequent lives, always striking out whenever he felt attacked.

There was a soul who formed part of a volcano at this crucial moment in our history. Her experience of the volcano was that she ended up being buried in a mountain of molten ash and was not able to survive. Her only conscious memory was that of being suffocated and buried. Subsequent incarnations have always held her in this same mould and she has re experienced the moment in differing guises, time and time again.

I have come across a few souls who were shepherds at the time. They have each been affected in differing ways, but usually these people have an issue with animals and are lonely, isolated types.

Quite often I come across souls who were animals caught up in some sort of huge frenzy. Some were unhappily being killed and some were the actual killers. Every time the soul and I 'see' the event that occurred it is always very dramatic.

Most of the souls I have come across so far, who have reached the point of being able to comprehend the 'split', are gentle souls. The ones who were violent at the moment of the split as yet shy away from these understandings, but they should not. No one could 'help' where they were at the time of the split and they should not be held responsible for actions that were unavoidable at the time. If we had known what was happening and could have reasoned our way through the event, we would probably all have behaved quite differently. But of course we had no idea and could not explain it.

No living thing should ever be held unforgivably accountable for anything they have done, for it was all done in ignorance and it is only ignorance that still holds them captive. Karma of course has to be completed and it may be that some souls can only complete their karma once they have understood where they were at the time of the split. There is no set order as to how we all progress.

We are all a part of the whole process and are therefore equally responsible for helping each other become free from our particular wounds. Our own circumstances happened because the planet reached a fifty/fifty balance and we happened to *be* 'wherever we happened to *be*'. The first moment of consciousness was terrifying for us all and the impact felt then and now should be released thoroughly with time, patience and unconditional love.

Many, many souls are now working through the various lives that they have had which have caused devastation and damage to their beings. When they finally come to the place where they can access their first experience of emotion they understand why everything has happened to them and in the knowing, they can set themselves free.

The importance of the Moment of Consciousness is further understood by knowing that many collections of souls today that were 'one soul' at the time of the split and experienced their first emotions as one, are reuniting again now, after many, many years of separation and different experiences. They are incarnating together at the present time in close proximity, for example, as family or friends, even workmates, some working from the non physical side and some from the physical. This is happening to enable them to recognise each other again and heal; the healing process allowing them all the opportunity to reach the root of their first emotions and allowing them to gain further understanding of our evolution.

The souls that are coming together are all helping each other in this deep healing process. Sometimes these souls show up as people we feel a discomfort with. But we need to encompass 'all' in our quest for understanding, because until 'all' who made up each unique soul at the time of the split are reunited and growing, we cannot heal ourselves fully. Our collective soul can only be as 'light' as the least soul in our group.

Some souls in our current lives are from beings that caused us terrible damage at the time of the split or are souls that we damaged. We have come together at this time to heal all the damage, to understand it, and to forgive it in all aspects. Each time this happens, more and more light returns to earth.

Taking these enormous thoughts one step further, our whole planet is only as evolved as the least evolved soul that exists. The more evolved souls must eventually pull the least evolved souls through the eye of the needle for, of course, we are all 'one' at source!

Chapter three

Balance explained

The next part of my narrative is the hardest to relate. This is because it is a personal account concerning Dom's actual death, both in physical and spiritual terms. He has shown much to me in order that I could achieve complete peace over his passing, and now he allows me to share it unselfishly with you. I say unselfishly because it does not show him up in a very good light, but by sharing it with as many people who can understand it as possible he will hopefully help some of you continue your own life journey in a much more enlightened way.

Dom enjoyed climbing. In August 2008 he was due to embark on a mountain leaders' course with the Royal Marines which would qualify him to train other people to climb. He decided to go and do some practise climbs, before the course, to get back in to the swing of things after breaking his arm and having a hernia operation.

He took off one sunny Sunday, accompanied by his younger brother and his girl friend. He chose a very picturesque spot, near the Devon coast, six miles from

Plymouth. After deliberating on which was the best place to ascend, he began his climb and reached his first destination safely, a ledge about sixty five metres above the ground. But as he started to abseil back down to ground level something happened and he fell. He landed on extremely rocky terrain, crashing his head on some sharp rocks and falling very quickly unconscious.

He survived in hospital for ten days, but did not regain consciousness before he died. The following is an account of what happened between my son and I during his last ten days.

When I entered the intensive care unit where Dom was lying, a few hours after his accident, I realised immediately that he wasn't in his body. His body was lying on a bed, heavily drugged to stop him moving, so I said to the Dom that I felt floating swiftly up and down the room,

"Dom, this is your body. It isn't a joke. You are actually looking at your own body. Go back in and see for yourself."

I felt him stop abruptly in his tracks and I felt a massive shock run through him. I heard his thoughts:

"Oh no, that can't be right"

So I said, "Yes, Dom. Go back in your body and have a look at the truth for yourself".

I felt him slide back into his body.

After a short while I left the room, to give him time to come to terms with the situation.

The next time I visited Dom he was safely back in his body and was taking on full recognition of what had happened. I knew I could not communicate with him at this point so I decided to leave him until he was ready to contact me.

Some time later, I forget which part of the hospital I was in, I felt Dom around me again. He wanted to discuss everything with me, which was quite natural to him when he was in trouble. He knew I could hear him because we had already communicated. We discussed the damage to his brain and the general physical state of his body. We discussed whether he could pull his body back from this situation in a way that he could live a future life with some sort of meaning. Having talked over every aspect, he then went off to consider it all and to see how he could go about healing himself.

Meanwhile his girl friend Eileen and I were offering his body healing, the doctors were keeping him stable with drugs and all that could be done to give him the best chance of recovery, including further operations, was happening.

Over the next few days I made it clear to Dom that he would only receive a full healing if he truthfully faced himself, faults and all. We discussed in detail, the main issues that troubled him in this life and he managed to face them all full on and accept them for what they were. He accepted that he had not handled them correctly and promised never to run away from them again. We faced character difficulties that he had and how he could put them right. These things were not achieved quickly. It took a lot of trust on his part and a lot of admitting. But it was not a new process. Dom and I had done many mini sessions like this in the past, but never before at such a deep level and with such intense sincerity. Dom knew that he had to lay himself completely bare if he was to have any chance of survival.

By the time the doctors decided to have an attempt at bringing Dom round, he felt ready to attempt a return to life. Over the next day or so his physical condition swung precariously and eventually, due to an infection, the doctors had to fully sedate him again.

I found myself back in communication with Dom. We discussed the possibility of him giving his life totally into the service of God. This might mean he could carry on as a Royal Marine…….but it might not. It might mean that he could live at his beloved farm again one day……….but it might not. It might mean he could keep his current girl friend………. but it might not. But giving his life to God and relinquishing all his earthly desires would mean that the highest good for humanity would be achieved, and Dom decided that whatever the cost to himself, this was what he wanted.

A little while later, I was sitting at Dom's bedside and I said to the nurse,

"It would take a miracle to help him now wouldn't it?"

She nodded slowly.

As I sat there I prayed as I had never prayed before. I asked God to show me healing in its deepest form. After a while I felt healing energy circulating the quietness of the room. I felt it surround Dom and I felt its power.

A little later, I went upstairs to the hospital chapel. As I entered, the atmosphere inside was overwhelmingly powerful. I can only attempt to describe it as thick, almost tangible, and as I walked further into the chapel I felt I might faint at any moment. I looked up at the plain wooden cross above the altar and I became aware that in that very moment Dom was giving his life to God in an 'unconditional' way. I plonked unsteadily onto a chair in front of the cross and felt the tears streaming down my face. I felt so incredibly proud of Dom. It was a moment like no other. I sat in silence and shared his private experience in awe. No one came in to disturb us.

I don't know how long I sat in the chapel for but after a while I felt the atmosphere clear a little and I managed to get up shakily and make my way back down stairs to Dom's unit. My emotions were swinging like billio at this point. Sometimes I felt that Dom was definitely going to live and sometimes I felt his body was too damaged and that he wouldn't manage to. But at all times I continued to pray that the highest good should happen, whatever that might be.

Shortly after this the doctors told us that they had controlled the infection in Dom's body and they had decided to have another go at pulling him back into consciousness. I felt that Dom was going to give living another go and I felt him slipping back into his body. I left him to it.

But the battle to heal his body had become too great by this time. A lot of his vital organs had started packing up and I think Dom realised that he was too damaged to have any decent future quality of life. After a further twenty four hours the doctors suggested turning the ventilators off and Dom died peacefully an hour later.

I knew that the process that Dom and I had been through whilst he was lying unconscious had completed most of the life objectives he had preset for this life. The content of our discussions had fast forwarded him so much that he had died quite spiritually grown. I felt terrific joy for him in that, because we had achieved the 'greater plan' if not the human desire!

The day after Dom's funeral I was lying outside in a long chair and I must have momentarily dropped off to sleep. I remember dreaming I was squatting on the edge of a small ledge with my face to the rock face and my back to the elements. I then felt my feet slip, first the left one and then the right, very specifically in that order. I thought I was falling and I woke up with a huge start. I immediately knew that Dom had been trying to show me how he fell. I rushed into the kitchen where Eileen was busy cooking and asked her what position she had last seen Dom in when he had been on the ledge. She said,

"Squatting."

So I had my confirmation. I was only later to realise how important this little incident was.

I had the overwhelming feeling that it had not been on Dom's blueprint that he was to die at this time. I suppose I kept asking the question,

"Why? Why did it happen?"

I felt a desperate need to know why I had lost the son that I had never suspected I would lose. I had been told that these were my last children many years ago and that I would be able to enjoy them to the full. What had happened? What

29

had changed and how could it? My mind never stopped. Many people visiting the retreat had ideas about it and told me that it was his time to go. I didn't believe them. It simply didn't feel right to me.

I have no need to go into detail about the events of the next few months because you already know that the revelations I have previously recounted were received during that period. The next thing I want to share with you really began around the time of the inquest some nine months after the accident.

Dom's girl friend, Eileen, came and stayed with me the night before the inquest. She reluctantly showed me the last picture that she had ever taken of Dom. It was taken twenty minutes before he died. She didn't like it and she wasn't sure why. I took one look at the photo and I was flabbergasted. It showed a picture of Dom and Eileen close together. The energy round Eileen looked vibrant and alive. The energy round Dom looked dark and closed. It was horribly apparent and when I pointed it out to Eileen she knew immediately what I meant. I said to her,

"He had already gone!"

We both then knew that at that point in time his death was already known, at some level. The picture did not look like Dom at all. I felt I never wanted to see it again.

The day of the inquest dawned and little did I know what an astonishing day it would prove to be. We arrived in Plymouth to find the Royal Marines parading round the town having just come back from a tour in Afghanistan. As we approached the court room in the centre of the town, Marines seemed to be everywhere, playing their band music and marching in long columns with crowds lining the streets, clapping and cheering. It was nothing to do with us of course but at the same time it felt like it was everything to do with us.

There was a Royal Marine mountain expert at the inquest who was drafted in by the court to give his opinion on how the accident happened. My younger son Edward and Dom's girl friend Eileen had to give evidence as to what they had witnessed on the day. It was to be the first full account of the accident the rest of the family had ever heard.

It transpired that the Royal Marine expert, from the evidence showing on the ground at the scene of the accident, thought that Dom had safely climbed up the rock face, being belayed by Edward. When he reached the top he put his two anchor points in, ran the rope between the anchor points and tied a knot. At this point he called to his brother that he was safe.

He busied himself up on the ledge for a while and the expert explained that at that stage, Dom would have probably realised that he couldn't abseil down because of the knot, so he would have tried to undo it. He said that it looked as if Dom had slipped at that point, the anchor points had failed to hold him and he had fallen. Both anchor points were found on the ground. It was evident to the Royal Marine expert that Dom had not put his anchor points in with a fifty/fifty weighting. He had put them in unevenly, which was why they had not held his weight and saved his life. A verdict of accidental death was given.

After the inquest we, the family, decided to go and visit the spot where Dom had fallen. We climbed over very rough terrain to the scene of the accident. I looked at the sharp rocks at the foot of the cliff, wondering which one had dealt the fatal blow. Then I looked up at the ledge from which Dom had fallen and to my amazement I could see him waving and smiling down at me from the top. He spoke clearly,

"This is the last thing I remember, mum. I don't remember being on the ground."

These were very comforting words for a troubled and grieving mum! He also let me know that he had been very happy in his last moments.

I looked up again at the ledge to which Dom had climbed. I could just make out where his anchor points would have been. I suddenly realised there was no way that Dom could have fallen from that ledge. There was a tree growing out from the centre and it would have caught him or at least made quite a noise of breaking branches as he fell past it, which neither his brother nor Eileen had heard. My glance slid to a foot below the ledge where there was a long crack in the rock running almost parallel to the ledge but on a distinct slant. The slant ran across the rock face, the left side lower than the right.

My brain started to turn crazy somersaults.

It became abundantly clear to me that Dom had started to abseil down the cliff face, realised the knot was stopping him, and put his feet in the convenient crack to take his weight and balance himself while he tried to undo the knot. Of course, the exact angle of the crack would mean that most of his weight would have been on his left foot! My brain tracked back to the dream I had had the day after the funeral. So that was why I had felt my left foot slide first and the right foot afterwards!

My gaze was riveted on the crack in my sudden comprehension.

My mind moved on.........The anchor points that should have held him were not placed in a balanced way and therefore did not hold him when his weight suddenly required it.

I felt incredibly sick.

I knew that I had come as close as anyone could, to knowing what had happened and why. Dom had given me such a distinct clue in that dream, the day after the funeral. And the anchor points were a *huge* sign that Dom was not balanced in his life. The opinion of the Royal Marine expert was given as a confirmation of this fact.

I am now going to ask you to bring back to mind the two walks which I took when I received the revelations. Having already been shown that this planet is all about balance from the moment of the split, I was now to learn how crucial balance is in every single aspect of creation. Everything has its own balance or pivotal point. The world is finely balanced on its axis, trees are finely balanced by their branches, finances are finely balanced though they have recently swung about precariously, honesty is a fine balance that we tread in every walk of life. I could go on and on........

The opposites that were created at the time of the split require us to keep both sides in our sights. When one side heavily outweighs the other it can be said that we are in a vulnerable position. Take the weather for example. If all the rain falls in one place it creates destruction on a massive scale. If no rain falls it can create a famine. When the planet is relatively balanced the weather takes on a more balanced role and we have a mix of rain and sun. Then everything flourishes. This 'weather' balance can occur on a world wide scale, a country size scale or simply a 'one town' scale, as witnessed recently all over the world

So............going back to Dom. It was with utter dismay that I suddenly realised he had been functioning from a vulnerable position. The tough life tests that he had experienced during the last two years had pushed him beyond a level that he could cope with. Therefore he had been living on the vulnerable side of his pivot point for the last few months but none of us had known it. I knew of course that he was being pushed very, very hard but I thought I would be able to help him gently over the coming years. I did not understand that once we are functioning on the vulnerable side of our pivot point, our survival is dependent on the will of the collective conscious.

In case you are wondering what a decent young man like Dom could have been doing to become so vulnerable I will explain:

Two years previously, Dom had had a short friendship with a young lady of a similar age to himself. It was nothing serious, he just took her out occasionally. She had previously been married and she told Dom that she couldn't have children. He, being a very trusting sort, believed her and took a silly risk by having unprotected sex. It didn't take Dom too long before he realised she was not the one for him and he told her he didn't want to take her out any more. Shortly afterwards he left for a tour in Afghanistan feeling that he was free to go his own way and so was she.

Little did he know that she was already pregnant. I will not go into any detail about what happened between them except to say that the situation being as it was, and my son being such a sensitive and trusting soul, the ensuing financial battle blew his mind into a terrible place.

Although I was very upset for my son, like any mother would be, I thought that I had plenty of time to help Dom accept the consequences of his former 'silly' actions. I thought I could one day help him accept that the baby was his and that he had a responsibility towards him. I was convinced that if I could persuade the young lady to leave Dom alone for a while he would calm down and I could help them both to see the situation in a more reasonable light. I had written to her explaining this but had not had a reply.

At this time Dom was coming home nearly every weekend. I knew it was because he needed refuge from what was going on and I didn't question him, feeling that his home should rightly be the refuge that he sought. However, he was obviously very bitter and was saying some pretty harsh things.

He didn't mean them of course, but he was at the time receiving phone calls during the night, and when he picked the phone up he could hear the baby screaming on the other end of the line. He was experiencing the mother hounding him at his flat on a regular basis. The more she hounded him, the angrier he became. He wouldn't talk about it to any of us.

He was shutting us, and it, out.

Around the end of April that same year, (about two months before Dom had his accident) I had felt an energetic change around the farm. I had also been told by the universe that my deceased mother had to go and do another job (in the spirit world) and I was informed that I would have a temporary guide. This temporary guide turned out to be a novice and I thought at the time that I was having her to give her an opportunity to work with someone like me.

Everything in my diary began to empty. I had just opened the retreat and was starting to take bookings. Suddenly no more bookings came in. I just had a few enquiries that came to nothing. My own personal diary became empty. I found myself wandering around the farm saying to the universe,

"Well, ok. I'm here if you need me but I accept it if you don't."

I was beginning to think that I wasn't going to run a retreat after all! However that seemed very strange, after all the work and finance that had gone into it. There was a kind of hush around me, and I didn't know why.

On June the twenty second Dom fell. It was immediately apparent to me why my life had come to a standstill. It was also immediately apparent that the universe had known from the end of April that Dom's time was near. He had, at that moment, crossed the fatal line; he was on the wrong side of his pivot point. He was vulnerable! My mother had withdrawn from me in order to prepare as much as she could, for the oncoming event.

From June the twenty second until the time he died, Dom was in the hands of the collective conscious. He was given time with me to come to terms with his situation which is exactly what he did. He was given the time to face himself and fulfil his life purpose before he died. At the moment he gave his life to God he was once more, finely balanced. If it had been in the highest interests of the collective conscious that he should make a full recovery that is what would have happened. If it had been in the highest interests that he should make a partial recovery, it would have impacted on his entire family in a different way, but that is what would have happened. But it was in the highest interests of the collective consciousness that he should die, so that is what did happen.

We, as mere mortals, can never know what the 'highest' good for the collective conscious can be. We cannot judge. We cannot see the bigger picture. But we can be aware of the highest good for ourselves, when we are balanced and centred.

The greatest message that Dom has brought us from the other side is to let us know what happened to him and why. Through the anchor points, he brought us factual proof, for if he had been 'balanced' he would have weighted his anchor points evenly. There is a tipping point for each of us, all of the time, and we can all become vulnerable if we don't redress the balance. Once in the hands of the collective conscious, we still have the chance to redress it in this life, unless we die first. You might ask why murderers live on for so many years after they have committed such an awful crime? I did! But of course the answer to serving in the highest way is not ours to know. The facts surrounding the murderer are not weighable by humans but they are weighed carefully by our spiritual counterparts and the best result allowed.

I did ask Dom why so many people came to the farm and told me it was his time to go. He said,

"We had to allow it mum. We had to make you question!"

He also confirmed to me that it had not been on his blueprint that he should die at this point and he has never ceased to apologise and to help me in every way he can. I do not ask this of him. He chooses to do this.

While I still miss my son very, very much, the peace that I have over his death is complete at every level. We now work together to bring this and other knowledge to those who are ready to hear. One of the other gifts it has brought is my fuller understanding of our total life path from source to the present day and how the knowledge of where we were at the time of the split is so crucial to healing our current emotions.

Chapter Four

My own Experience of the Split

'Fear *is* the unknown'.

I have been slowly putting together my own experience of the 'split'. Different pieces of it have been shown to me at different times and I still don't know if there is more to come. However it currently runs something like this:

At the exact moment of the split I was in my mother's womb. She was seven months pregnant. I believe I was human.

My first memory was a stifled feeling of trying to breathe through my nose and finding that I could not. I remember becoming aware that I was confined tightly in a small, soft, dark, fleshy space and knowing that the environment in which I was held was somehow altering. I became aware that it was dark and I was trapped. I recall the unexpected shift from the peace, love, security and calm that I had been experiencing as quite the norm, to the onset of confusion and fear. I felt it through my mother's womb whilst at the same time I still felt protected and safe. I know I 'logged' this change and I strained every nerve and sinew to try and understand what had happened. But somehow I recognised that it was hopeless to try and understand 'why' everything was changing. I simply remember knowing that I could do nothing about it at that moment and I just had to experience the change from where I was. I was left in a state of confusion and worry but I totally trusted that all would be well.

Two months later I was born and I remember emerging into this changing world, feeling very lost and vulnerable without my mother's protection and thinking to myself,

"This wasn't what I was expecting. Where am I? Where is my world? What has happened?"

Nothing felt right. My mother felt familiar but she was tense and ill at ease. I could hear lots of different noises and feel 'worry' all around me. My surroundings appeared dark and I could feel a consuming and overwhelming fear. I smelt death but I didn't know what it was. Everything seemed amiss and I didn't know why. In my heart I was searching...........searching. Where was the 'light'?

A couple of months or so after my birth, I remember I was dozing in a type of leafy hammock which was hanging from a tree. I woke up to see a *massive* lion approaching the place where I was hanging. He raised himself up to his full height at the sight of the 'light' and from this position, close to my face, I heard him emit the most enormous roar. The emotion I felt emanating from the lion was an all encompassing, ferocious anger. I was somehow aware of my mother running from the scene. I started screaming and the lion tore me to pieces.......

And that was it! I guess I was eaten! I certainly passed swiftly back to the other side.

Explanation:

Because of 'where I happened to be', at the time of the split, I actually incarnated on that occasion as 'light'. Therefore I was one of the first beings to incarnate as light, after the split. Nor did I live long enough in that lifetime to become totally swamped by the 'dark'.

When the lion saw me he was immediately filled with anger at the sight of 'light' and his anger made him attack. He felt a great need to extinguish the light, and this need was driven by fear. So in his fear, he overpowered the light. The lion, for those of you who have read my first book, was Derek.

When Derek towered over me in a similar way in this life, of course I relived the terror of that first conscious incarnation and that is obviously why I almost died. He appeared to tower above me in his anger as he had done so long ago as a lion, although neither he nor I were conscious of this at the time. But I now realise that something in our conversation must have triggered an old memory and he started attacking the 'light' in the same way.

The emotions that I listed when I was in the womb are very much key emotions that I have lived with all this lifetime..........

I have lived this and probably all my other lives feeling trapped inside my skin. I have for some time felt that my skins were gradually releasing but of course did not realise that I was actually releasing the moment of the split. The most important aspect of this is that I have been blaming my own skin for the trapped feeling and now I know that it was my mother's womb that was 'apparently' trapping me and that *my* skin was never a trap. Therefore I can live in my own skin happily now. I also realise why I felt so lost and vulnerable when my mother died in this life. I have always felt the need to be cradled, protected and loved by a mother because that was how I felt in my mother's womb at the first moment of the split. But now I can stand alone, understanding at the deepest level where those strong emotions came from.

I recognise that throughout all my lives I have been desperate to bring the light back to earth. I have been confused by the world around me. I have felt the fear in the same way as I did back then and I have known that it shouldn't be that way. I have longed for the world that I remembered, the world before the split.

I have always been wary of small tight spaces, but not allowed myself to be overcome by them. Therefore I can ride in lifts but I have to detach myself from the 'perceived' danger in order to do it. I can go into small spaces like attics, but with difficulty. I am unable to go underwater with any ease at all. I hate the feeling of water filling my nose. I used to think it was because I had drowned in a past life but I now know for sure that it is a similar feeling to the one which I had at the initial moment of consciousness in the womb (the unable to breathe feeling.)

I have always been puzzled by the world and expected it to be something that it isn't. I always naively trust everyone and go around with an innocence that is quite ridiculous for my age. I know now that I live constantly as I did the moment after I was born in that first conscious life. I feel that energy, I live that energy, I am that energy...................

and I am always searching through the confusion of 'life' for answers. And then, when something 'black' comes at me………I tend to 'die' inwardly………….just as I did, so long ago.

The understanding of these events has helped me to understand myself, my purpose and my journey through my lifetimes, so much better. I get stronger and clearer with each moment.

My personal part of the current 'great plan' came about because of where I was at the time of the split. I formed part of the 'light' energy that finally achieved an incarnation as 'Noah'. Each and every one of us will be dominated by our first emotions until we understand them and move through them. This is part of the great ascension process that is bringing more and more light back to our planet.

In one of my first incarnations after the split I can remember living in a dark, damp cave. The cave was a very basic home with carcasses strewn around the floor and skeletons hanging on the walls. Derek was my husband/partner and I could sense that we had a few children. He was the bread winner and he spent a lot of his time out hunting. I was left alone all day, looking after the children. I recall that we did not wear much in the way of clothing, mainly animal skins round our groins.

One day he came home and I can remember I was crying for some reason. He raised the weapon he was holding, his whole body was full of an unreasonable anger, and he killed me.

The importance attached to remembering this life is because of what happened afterwards. When we had both once more returned to the non-physical side, we reviewed what had happened between us. We both understood that in order to help heal the world and ourselves, we would have to heal all the emotions that we had both incurred, throughout both those lifetimes. This would have to be done over a number of incarnations, but we both made a firm pact that this is what we would do. We knew it would always be a form of 'light meeting dark' and that each time we met things would be very, very hard, but when our mission was complete, in some way our bit of light would be returned to the planet.

When Derek 'towered over me' on that fateful day during this life, and I reacted the way I did, we were in fact completing one of the last pieces of our jigsaw. We were bringing the first incident of the lion back to the fore and we were doing it because I was in an evolved enough state to comprehend the situation and would therefore be able to heal the past for ever.

I have indeed understood our story though as yet I have not been able to tell Derek. Whether I ever do or not is irrelevant to me for only the universe knows the timing of Derek's needs. However, my full understanding of the story brings full release of that part of the dark energy that was created at the time of the split. Light has finally conquered darkness as it always will and now there is nothing but love remaining.

The importance of sharing this information is because so many other people at this moment are meeting similar counterparts. Light energies are choosing to incarnate and dwell amongst relevant dark energies in order to bring healing to bear from the time of the split. These brave souls who are trying to bring light to our planet in the most painful of circumstances are not allowing the dark energy to 'win'. Men and women are finally having to stand up to each other at this very deep level; the level of the split.

The dark *is* thinning and light *is* returning.

And so I return to the statement 'Fear *is* the unknown'

When I was sitting in my mother's womb in love, peace, security etc, I didn't know it. I only knew it when the split altered all our sensations. Then, and only then, I could look back and see what I had been. So I have to bless the *hell* that became our earth at that time and furthermore I bless the fact that we are bringing heaven (light) ever closer again, this time knowing what we are doing.

Chapter Five

Another soul shares her experience of the split

I have already told you that, where we were, at the time of the split is extremely important. Add to that...... who we were, why we were, what we were and, the knowledge of whether we were incarnate or in spirit. But more important than anything else, as we come to understand the moment of the split, is to *experience* the moment for ourselves, once more. It is only in the personal re-experiencing of our own moment that we come to understand just what that moment did to us, and at the same time it will help us understand the moment that light entered the planet at source.

For me, living this moment and re experiencing it brought a feeling of *understanding* the planet and its purpose such as I had never known before. It also brought a personal understanding of my own journey. I saw the connection between the moment when the light became trapped at source and the moment when I became consciously 'trapped' in the womb. And I understood the illusion of it all at an even greater depth. As I emerged from the womb, the 'light' I met gave me a feeling of recognition of what I thought had been taken from me when I was in the womb. I 'saw' the light for the first time and I mistakenly started to look outward for the light.

And then I understood! I recognised that it was an illusion. I knew 'I' was the light, I always had been, and that the planet we could see through our eyes, smell, touch, hear etc. was an illusionary playground.

When people come to see me I always know when they are ready to explore who or what they were at the time of the split. As we begin by asking the universe for clarification of their story the person involved quite often sinks into a state where they can relive the experience for themselves. More often than not I sink with them and this helps enable the person to have the confidence to go 'all the way'.

Every time I have been privileged to share this experience with someone the moment has been extraordinary. They suddenly come to understand so much about themselves and see the trend of their lifetimes and why things have happened. One such person has very kindly agreed to share her experience with us here:

In her own words…………………

"I had known for some time that I needed to start tackling the reason why I could not feel 'love'. I had never been in touch with love and despite tackling many other areas of imbalance in my life I had never faced this aspect. I started asking the universe for help. And help came……………

I called at the farm to collect some boots that I had left behind on a previous visit. I was talking to Anna about something that had happened recently with a friend of mine and somehow our conversation got deeper and deeper. She had been offering for several months to have a session with me as she could detect that all was not well. In the past these sessions have often been uncomfortable and I have never felt totally at ease with them. I felt I was nearly always the 'bad guy' and having to accept home truths that I would rather not acknowledge. I had been putting off the current problem sensing that it was very deep and quite frankly I was scared. My life seemed quite comfortable and settled thank you very much and the last thing I wanted was another major soul searching upset.

Perhaps because we hadn't arranged anything, but in retrospect, more likely because the universe had answered my prayers and we had been thrown together at exactly the right moment, I didn't brush Anna off. She started by saying that my aura was grey and asked if I would like help in working out what the problem was. I knew I wasn't at ease with myself so I said,

"Yes".

She sunk into a trance state and said almost straight away that she could see me on a hillside. I was a shepherd with a crook in my hand and my sheep were scattered all over the hills surrounding me. She could not sense any other human around but she could feel the tremendous empathy and telepathic communication that I had with my sheep.

As Anna described this scene I felt an immense association with it. It felt very familiar. I have always loved walking alone amongst the sheep in the mountains of Wales. I have often said I would like to live in the Welsh mountains with a dog and with a mountain to climb right outside my front door. I also adore my sister's two dogs and have a special relationship with them. I can't bear to see any animal in pain but I would love to have an animal of my own one day. I have only recently realised that I have never had sole responsibility for any animal and how scared I am of the emotional attachment that owning an animal would entail.

As Anna spoke I felt such a warm comfortable feeling of recognition. It was as if she was describing something that I remembered doing in this life. I really did feel as if she was telling me about my life and the really amazing thing was that I could associate with the feeling of loving my sheep and being at one with them. It was a feeling I could never remember having experienced before. It was wonderful!

Then Anna said she could sense something momentous happening. I had a vision of a wolf coming and taking one of my sheep. Anna continued without knowing about my vision. She said,

"I can feel something so big and painful about to happen that it's almost unbearable. It's something along the lines of a loss of trust between you and your sheep."

As she was speaking I felt it as blame. Something had happened to one or more of my sheep and I felt them all looking at me with accusing eyes. I had failed to protect them! She then said in a rather awed voice, that she thought she was seeing the moment of the 'split' as it had occurred in my life.

I realised Anna was describing my loving and happy life being shockingly disrupted as the split occurred, robbing me and my sheep of all that we knew, as we became conscious.

I was immediately faced with accusing eyes, loss of trust, and loss of oneness and love. It felt as if I had subsequently struggled through all the rest of my lives looking for that love and never regaining it.

All this resonated very deeply within me. I felt able to accept that something had happened many lives ago that had appeared to remove love from my life. It was such a relief to realise that there was a reason *why* I struggled so much and that it wasn't my fault.

Anna then stood in front of me and said,

"Try and see what else you can remember from that life."

I immediately saw a very bright light a long way into the distance. It was like a small torch burning very strong and white. I described it to her.

She asked,

"What do you think that light is?"

The phone rang at that moment, giving me a chance to consider her question. My initial thought was that the light was God. I think this was conditioned by books I have read about near death experiences where people walk towards bright lights. I then thought that maybe the light was 'love'.

When Anna came off the phone I told her this and she said to me,

"Try and see which way the light is flowing. Is it flowing away from you or towards you?"

I detected a flow and in rather a forlorn voice said,

"It's going away from me."

A moment later I said,

"Oh! That's the right way!"

The love was actually flowing outwards from me to the 'great outside'!

I cannot tell you what a dramatic moment that was. It was the very first time in this lifetime that I felt I had the ability to love! I actually felt love inside me and it was able to flow out to others. Anna told me that it had been there all the time but it had got blocked in. My body was racked with sobs of joy and amazement. The dog on my lap must have wondered what was going on as I hugged him and kissed him on the top of his head. I can remember saying to Anna that it was as if a block of ice somewhere inside me (I think in my heart area) was cracking.

Shortly after this I drove home and I asked the universe to protect me as I had nearly driven into another car at the bottom of Anna's driveway! I drove along feeling love for *everything*. I loved the fields, the trees, the sky............I loved everything I looked at. I gave thanks to God of course and felt such an abundance of love in my heart that it was almost overwhelming. I mused that if a policeman stopped me I would probably just smile at him and possibly even thank him if he gave me a ticket!

Later that day, and the next day, anyone I met got a hug. When I was asked how I was, I would say,

"Absolutely brilliant, on top of the world, thank you"

I smiled at everyone and sent love to everyone I thought of.

It was a couple of days later that I got the first attack of diarrhoea. I had eaten soup at lunch time and wondered if it had been a bit rich. It seemed unlikely as four of us had eaten the soup and only I was affected. But something caused me to dash to the loo three times in quick succession! For the next week or so I continued to have loose bowels. I was not ill in any way and I could only assume that it was a part of my emotional release.

I know that nothing can ever take away what happened to me that day. I now often feel the abundance of love within me and I ask God every night to help me allow it to grow. The experience has changed me in other ways too and my prayer is that the ice in my heart will continue to melt until it has all gone."

At some point we will all reach an understanding of the moment of the split, to a greater or lesser degree. We may describe it in other words, but that doesn't matter. What does matter is that we move safely through the moment and it will take us both backwards and forwards simultaneously, on our life path.

Chapter six

Some interesting extras

The following are some interesting episodes that have taken place between myself and Dom that people have found useful and therefore I have included them in these writings.

The apple

Dom has shown me that our planet can be likened to an apple.

When you look at an apple and you see it in all its glory, it is round, green, shiny, wholesome etc. If you imagine all the air and the water taken out of the apple it would shrivel to less than half the size.

If you were to suck the 'spiritual' out of the world we live in it would become less than half the size.

Spiritual and physical cohabitate to form our planet as we know it, as do the water and matter which form the apple.

Actually it's an interesting thought that perhaps the earth literally has expanded as emotion pushed its way to the surface. Perhaps it really was originally half or even quarter of the size!

Windows

During the first few days after Dom passed over, he showed himself to me by waving from one of the house windows. Then, in a fleeting second, he appeared in all the house windows, one after the other. I heard him say,

"Look mum! Look how fast I can move now!!"

I shrieked with laughter. It was so typical of him to share something like that.

Another joke

One day I was walking between the Cedar and the Beech tree in my garden and I could feel Dom and my mum in the Beech tree. I said to Dom,

"Dom, why are you always in the Beech tree and not in the Cedar?"

He replied, "Gran can't climb the Cedar!"

The cedar tree has an enormous fat trunk which no one can climb easily! Dom used to climb it with ropes but, to my knowledge, my mum had never been up it. I just loved his sense of humour and I loved the natural way which he referred to my mum as 'Gran'.

Communication

The normal way in which Dom speaks to me when he is around is testimony to the fact that he lives in exactly the same way now as he did when he was in his body. The only difference is I can't see him. He does however slide around his life line and isn't always in his 'last life' mode. Sometimes I feel him as I knew him in this life but sometimes I know it's him around but where he is speaking from is not necessarily a place that I know. By speaking to me from a different plane, he can teach me all sorts of different things.

He often helps me, from a different plane, to help people who come to see me. He needs to, in order to help that person for the best. He is learning to help people in a better and better way, and if he doesn't know the answer to a question straight away I feel him shoot off, (just as he used to in this life) to get the answer.

More recently Dom has been communicating from what one might call an even broader space. Apparently, because I was asking for deeper insight into the time before this planet began, he has shot off into that and communicates to me from there. So sometimes when I feel him, it is not in a personal way but in a 'general' way. But I still know it's him. And also, because I am pursuing knowledge and constantly asking him to help me, Dom is able to grow on the other side in a way that he would not be able to, if I didn't ask him.

More about general balance.

We are *so* expendable. As long as we are of use to 'evolution', in other words, on the *right* side of our pivot point, all will progress in our life. When we become useless through our own stubbornness to progress we become so expendable. The universe actually doesn't care. If we die we are simply moving on to where we *can* be useful. The bigger picture doesn't see things like we do. All this 'desire' to save a life is a pointless exercise to the bigger picture. The only important thing is progressing on our path in what we might call spiritual terms. (All this was quite a shock to me when I first realised it.)

Asking to be balanced is a hugely important prayer we can use and it is currently little used. If we ask to be balanced we will always be moving towards 'growth'. If we sit ignorantly imbalanced we are vulnerable. Just knowing this will change our lives. Knowing it as explained from the source of this planet helps us see it at a much deeper level. This is such a huge gift of understanding that Dom brings us.

Also understand that balance runs through the centre of every existence and every part of existence. A cake has to be made with carefully balanced ingredients in order to give the best result. A business has to be balanced in order to succeed. As individuals we need to be balanced in order to grow safely.

This is a time to fine tune our balance at every level. Wherever we are or whoever we are we each have different pivot points relevant to ourselves. We can only work from our own pivot point, not from any one else's.

One great certainty that has solidified in me since the revelations is the deep and positive knowledge that there is nothing new about anything. It is *all* progress. It has always been progress and it will always be progress.

My holiday

During August 2010 I had a particularly busy week at the retreat. A lot of people were coming and going and I was cooking lunch for an elderly guest every day. I had one guest who I needed to be constantly tuned in to, I had my other guests' needs to attend and I was exhausted.

A friend offered to come and look after *me* for a couple of days to allow me to take a break from the daily chores in my own house! This sounded a wonderful idea and I was just about to work out how this could be accomplished when an astonishing thing happened.

I was walking through the 'magic woods' where all my other revelations have taken place when I felt Dom join me. I was delighted as I had not felt him so vividly for a long time.

Firstly he told me that if he had been alive we would have been going on a holiday to the Swiss Alps together. I mentioned that we had planned to do this the previous year (a year after he died) but he simply said,

"It wouldn't have happened then, mum! We would have gone at this time instead."

I didn't disbelieve him. Things are regularly changing in our family's plans.

As I walked along I started to recall the holiday that we had already had together in the Swiss Alps, one year before he died. It was such a wonderful memory that I often thought back to it, sometimes very tearfully and sometimes very happily. On this occasion I had not been thinking about it for very long before I realized that Dom was trying to tell me that this experience was different. He said,

"Come with me, mum!"

I wasn't sure what he meant but I felt he was surrounding me and taking me to the Alps. Suddenly we seemed to be at the top of a mountain looking down at a village below us. I went back into my memory and remembered the beautiful views that we had seen on our holiday. Dom was communicating that this was a different view. I looked again and I saw that it was! He said,

"Do you want to slide down the mountain on your bum?"

I said, "We will bump into poles and pine trees and things."

Dom replied, "No mum! Just slide and trust! You don't need to worry about hitting things in my world. You just trust that you will be safe and you will be safe".

The next instant I felt myself sliding down the mountain. The wind was loud in my ears and the sensation of sliding really fast was exhilarating. All too soon I reached the bottom.

Dom and I found ourselves on the outskirts of a pretty village. We walked along a narrow, snow covered lane, towards the centre. I glimpsed a carpenter's shop with simply designed wooden benches outside the door. At this point I slipped back into memory and remembered some of the shops we had seen on our first holiday together. Dom gently got my attention.

"Mum! Your first thought was correct. We are walking past a carpenter's shop!"

I managed to let go of the memory and slip back next to Dom on our new holiday. We passed a tiny bakery and I saw and smelt all the fresh croissants and bread in the window. Smelling them and just being aware of the baker's shop seemed to be enough. I asked Dom,

"Is this how it is for you? Do you simply walk past and go through the sensations?"

He replied, "Yes, exactly that! And you can have the sensations to the highest degree possible. Isn't it wonderful?"

And I had to agree that it was my finest ever experience of walking past a bakery.

Next Dom asked if I would like to go to the top of the mountain that we could see ahead of us. I looked consideringly at it, wondering for a fleeting second if I could make it to the top at Dom's pace.

He said, "Its ok mum. Just relax into it and we'll go together."

I suddenly found myself engulfed in a rush of air and ascending rapidly up the mountain side. We travelled so fast that we seemed to be at the top in no time. The mountain summit was covered in snow. I looked about me and once again slipped back into 'human' memory of a ski-ing holiday that the family had once had. Dom gently nudged me back and I saw again the view that was really ahead of me. A scene that was completely new to me was in front of my eyes. It was simply beautiful. Snow capped peaks and tree filled valleys as far as the eye could see.

Dom asked, "Would you like to ski down mum?"

I'm not a good enough skier" I replied.

"Just imagine the best skier that you have ever seen and that is who you will be," came Dom's response.

I imagined a skier that I had once seen on television. The next thing I knew I was ski-ing rapidly down a very steep slope, twisting and turning, cornering and sliding, wind rushing through my hair and past my face, leaving me feeling absolutely exhilarated. I didn't want it to end.

Dom took me next to the peak of a very high mountain. Just as we approached the top I said to Dom,

"We can't go to the top of this one. It's too foggy."

Indeed, we couldn't see the top. It was wrapped in a complete blanket of thick cloud. Dom said to me,

"This is the best bit of all, mum. This is one of the few times in my world when I can be completely alone. No-one can see me unless they happen to pass by and enter the cloud. You and I can be relatively alone and it is one of the only ways on my side that we can have some degree of privacy."

I was amazed and the story of Moses came into my mind and I resolved to look it up when I got home.

Dom asked if I would like a ride on a cloud. He found us a small one and we sat with our feet dangling over the edge. Our cloud took us gently over the beautiful mountains and valleys. By this time I had completely stopped fighting the experience and I sat contentedly watching the scenery go by. The sun shone on our backs, gently warming us and casting its glow over the mountains as we passed them.

Dom said quietly in my ear,

"This is where I spend a lot of my time mum. This is where I'm happy."

I found myself once more on my walk. The dogs were running along beside me and there were grey clouds above me. I felt in awe of what had just happened and I couldn't stop thanking Dom. I felt as if I had been on the holiday of a lifetime. I felt so rested and ready for the challenges that lay ahead.

My holiday had taken ten minutes (in our time) but it rejuvenated me completely. Since then I have not looked back. I have also felt very privileged to experience a little of Dom's current reality.

Chapter seven

Dragged, Kicking and Screaming.......

For the last few months I have been asking the universe to help me understand what was happening in the world before the split. Little did I know that my first lesson would be so dramatic and I shall share a little bit with you to give you an insight as to where this part of my journey is taking me. It starts as a narrative and changes to a diary.

Learning about Nourishment

The first nourishment came from the desire of evolving matter/light to aid other evolving matter/light to travel, without an apparent root to source.

Nourishment was originally absorbed through the skin as moisture. It was transmitted from one living source (such as grass) to the travelling source (such as the worm) believing that this would be the only way that the worm could travel without dying. Thus a 'dependency' emotion was created.

From this first 'devouring of each other' the eating dependency has evolved. The first worms and maggots absorbed mostly water but also picked up the essence of the plants, thus merging the two together for ever in a new way.

The merging continued because the experiment appeared to work. The worm successfully arrived at its destination and the evolving world began a new era in its development. Creation began to enjoy its merging and the essences that had developed independently from source, lost their immediate purity.

In the excitement of the moment, the merging idea took hold and many other mergers took place very quickly. Hence all types of new creatures started to evolve and they started to develop means of excretion………or…………. a means of sifting through what they absorbed. Their bodies started to keep what they thought they needed and to discard what they didn't…………………………..

It had never crossed my mind that one day I would be considering living without eating. Eating was something I did because I thought that I had to. It wasn't something I thought about much other than if I ate properly and in a balanced manner I would be healthy and have enough energy for what I wanted to do. I also enjoyed sitting in front of the television with a bar of chocolate or some peanuts on a cold winter's evening. I had never been fussy over food, basically producing for the family the same plain nourishing fresh diet that my mother had always produced for me. I had no interest in cooking other than that it was something

I had to do for the family on a daily basis. Shopping for food had always been a chore but was something that was unavoidable and therefore I just got on with it.

I suppose I first became aware of food in a different way when I opened the retreat. I was astonished to find how many differing milks there were on the market. For someone who had only ever experienced milk from a cow supplied in milkman sized bottles (apart from when my son was a baby and was allergic to it so he substituted it with orange juice!) the array of milks that turned up in my fridge was a real eye opener. I quickly realized that I could not cope with this level of diversity so I continued to supply cows milk in semi skimmed form for the guests and left it up to them as to whether they used it or not.

I used to supply fine brown bread from the bakers which I felt was suitable for incoming guests but then realized that at least half of them couldn't eat wheat. Couldn't eat wheat? What was this? My brain was struggling to compute!

And slowly, as more and more guests came to the farm with their weird and wonderful diets, my eyes were opened to the mass of foods, (and substitutes) that are available in this country today. Inside, I was always secretly amused at their dietary peculiarities though I never let it show. I witnessed long conversations about food at the farmhouse kitchen table and hardly ever joined in. It just wasn't my scene.

My awakening to the fact that we could exist without food came in quite a roundabout way in the early part of 2010. I was looking through the Cygnus magazines for a book called 'Living on Light' which I had seen in a previous edition but I couldn't find it so I rang Cygnus and asked if they were still stocking it. They didn't seem to know what I was talking about at the time but in the next issue of the magazine I noticed the book had been advertised. I was amused, realizing that the universe had probably prompted Cygnus to feature it.

So, I ordered it. .... and it never reached my friend!!!!

That week I was going on a small holiday for three days and I decided to take the book with me. I think I had only read a few pages when I realized that existing without food was quite possibly a step I was going to take in the future. The author talked about a 'twenty one day process' in which one goes through a three stage transition in order to start living off light. The stages involve: completely not eating for the first seven days, drinking a little water during the second seven days and drinking a little more during the third seven days. By the time this process is over he talked about the body having made a complete transition and being able to live permanently off light. I decided then and there to cut out breakfast and see how I felt.

Cutting out breakfast was one of the most dramatic decisions I had made for a while. For one thing it wasn't a carefully thought out decision and for the other it was done so completely on the spur of the moment. But it proved to be a massive learning curve that took me months and months to come to terms with.

As I was on holiday with two friends and we were staying in a hotel that didn't do breakfast, cutting out the meal was initially quite easy. What was not so easy was the fact that I had always felt that if I didn't eat regularly I would get very weak. This thought consumed me the whole of that first morning, so I asked continually that I should be fed from source (as mentioned in the book I was reading) and I was totally surprised to find that I did not lose any energy all morning and by lunchtime I was still feeling absolutely fine but very hungry indeed. I wolfed down my lunch in relief and as I had decided that I wouldn't hold back for the rest of the day, I ate anything and everything I wanted.

This pattern continued for the rest of the holiday and I continued to read the book, learning more and more about Michael Werner's journey. By the end of the holiday I said to my friends,

"I have no idea if I am really going to do this but I am going to go without breakfast for the summer and I may or may not take it further when the retreat closes in October. I know that right now, I am still struggling too much after the death of my son, and I am not strong enough to do this, but I may well be strong enough by the autumn."

And we left it at that.

Coming home and continuing this process was very odd. I lay in bed every morning and asked the universe to sustain me from the light source and trusted that it would happen. I was continually amazed that I never ever ran out of energy though I was always ravenous by lunchtime.

My thoughts at this time were all over the place. Panic in many ways, set in. I didn't really want to live without my favorite foods for the rest of my life. I suddenly discovered that I really *loved* chocolate after all and I started buying loads of chocolate Easter eggs. (I mean three small ones a week but that was loads for me!) I started buying all the things that I loved eating, thinking to myself,

"I've got to eat these now because before long I may not be able to eat them again."

Food took on a whole new meaning. Food suddenly became very important! Very important indeed!

I plodded on with life. I continued to do without breakfast and a mid morning snack and I continued to eat whatever I wanted during the rest of the day, mostly snacking like billio during the evenings. I never once lost energy! I continued to drink whatever I wanted to at any time.

The most important part of this exercise was that I was training my mind and body to understand that I ate food in the first place and that I may not eat it in the future. For someone who had put so little importance on food this was a very big learning curve indeed.

The universe, in its clever way, sent a guest to the retreat who had already been through the 'twenty one day process' suggested by Michael Werner in his book, as a way to learn how to 'live from light'. She seemed very pleased that I understood about her process at all and was more than happy to share her experiences. My youngest son, Edward, and I listened to her while she related her story and we were both very amazed at how easily she spoke about it. I was also very surprised that Edward took such an interest and it became obvious that he too might decide one day to live on light.

Meeting this lady and having her to stay for a week was hugely encouraging to me because I could see first hand that the process could be possible for me. It also gave me someone to talk about it with and some experienced support should I decide to go ahead with the process. I thanked the universe profoundly. A second guest turned up who also claimed to live without eating and I found that I didn't need to talk to him at all. I had my inner trust and all the information that I wanted for that moment.

By the autumn I had grown completely used to not eating until lunch time. I had got through hay making without any trouble, I had managed the retreat through all its busy periods and I was getting less and less ravenous at lunch times. I had never once flagged during the morning and in fact, I felt very well.

I started to think about the next stage I should go through. My mind had by this time thoroughly got used to the idea that I could live off light. I didn't really want to do it but my instinct told me that it was the next step in my ascension process and it could be very helpful. It felt as if the universe had definitely pointed me in this direction because it was something I needed to do in order to become 'lighter' and to enhance my connection to source.

By this time my body was starting to feel uncomfortable if it had lots of food in it. I was aware of excreting food as soon as possible because I didn't like the feeling it gave me. I became increasingly aware of the unnecessariness of the whole digestive process.

I began thinking seriously about what I should do. I read a book written by Jasmuheen, who had undergone the twenty one day process in nineteen ninety three and is now an expert on the subject. She described the process she went through in detail and how it impacted on her then and now. I was making plans. I told my son I was going to do the twenty one day process just after Christmas when our family/ guests had gone. I asked him if he would look after me. I felt very daunted by the whole thing and yet was feeling an increasing determination to go through with it. I decided to cut out all the snacks I was having in the evenings as my next preparation.

I read the twenty one day process again. I was uncomfortable. Something wasn't sitting right. Did I really need to go through this process? Couldn't I just gradually cut out food? Did I really have to go through this major trauma? I felt I had had enough traumas in my life and it wasn't making sense to go through another.

I thought seriously about the revelations that I had received. I thought about the journey that the first worms had made from one tree to another. I remembered how the grass had called out to the worms,

"Eat me! Absorb me! I will help you make the journey"

I felt strongly that we didn't really need to eat............. not because we could live off light but because we had initially started eating because we thought we were separated from source when we first left that first tree. It was an illusion. We are source! We don't need to absorb each other to survive. We don't need to eat each other. We just ARE!

The next day I was due to go for a day long walk with some friends. Strangely I didn't have an opportunity to eat anything until four thirty that day. I did not run out of energy and I felt a little hungry but otherwise not too bad. I kept telling myself,

"Eating is a habit! You know perfectly well you don't need to eat."

In fact I didn't have a proper meal that day at all and went to bed feeling very light.

The following morning I was due to play a tennis match at ten o'clock. During the first few games of the first set I suddenly realized that it was the first time that I had ever done anything competitive without eating breakfast. I then panicked when I remembered that I had not eaten much at all the day before. I told myself quietly,

"It's ok. Eating is an illusion. You don't need food."

I asked for help from the universe and almost immediately I started to play tennis in an incredible way. I could suddenly hit the ball strongly and beautifully. My reactions were so fast and I had plenty of energy. I felt fantastic. After a first very tight, very demanding set, I started to wobble. I thought,

"I can't do this again!"

And the second set was full of an internal argument with myself as to whether I could or couldn't do it again. I still played very well but the internal argument took the edge off things. I began to feel light headed and a little as if I couldn't see clearly so I said to the universe,

"Please help me have the energy I need to do this."

Straight away I felt better and my vision cleared.

I WAS BEING FULLY SUPPORTED!!!

After that set I succumbed to the pressure and ate four jaffa cakes (basically the only food to hand!) I then played a further two sets with no trouble at all and I played the best tennis I could ever remember playing.

All the way home I didn't feel hungry. I was really quite stunned. Could my tennis have been affected by my increasing dependence on the universe to sustain me? I had been so quick. My reactions had been so improved. I felt so good! I felt so clear!

That evening I started to suspect that I may not need to go through the twenty one day process at all. I was starting to feel as if my body already knew all it needed to know and that it was going to be a simple process of gradually cutting down on my food intake and clearing myself totally of the illusion that I needed to eat to survive.

Living off light?

I *am* the light.

Monday 22 November

I've made a decision! I'm going to stay with just the two meals a day for a little while. Then, I'm going to cut it down to one. Then, if I haven't cut it all out by Christmas I will go ahead and finish it off with my own version of the twenty one day process. I don't intend to give up drink yet, if ever! I can't see the need. This is not about 'proving' that one can live off light for me, for I already know that I can. I think this is about becoming lighter or getting clearer and nearer to oneness.

I'm now living very much from moment to moment. I am not trying to put exact timings on things, as just the outline as above is enough. Taking one day at a time is much less worrying for me.

I do hate the way this process is so all-consuming but I can't see any way around it. We are so programmed to eating. It is such a very hard habit to stop!

Thursday 25th November

I am now getting quite used to only eating twice a day and not snacking at all. I am starting to eat lighter and less and my energy is so far quite high. In fact I feel really well with no weight loss that I can tell (trousers fit around the waist in the same way.)

I went shopping today. I waved at the foods that I normally buy and said,

"Hello" and "thank you" to them.

I seem to be going long hours without eating, quite successfully and not even feeling hungry when it is my allotted time to eat. But I do feel the need to tread carefully and to do this little by little and with the least possible fuss.

Friday 26th November

I ate some chocolate yesterday evening. It was really interesting because when I got into bed I felt uncomfortable and could actually feel the chocolate sitting heavily inside me. I mustn't do that again. I didn't feel right again until lunch time today when my energy shot up again. When I went for a walk this afternoon I got up the hills very easily.

Normally it's quite a struggle and I'm used to a struggle. It felt odd to shoot up the hill without the struggle! It seems the less I eat the better my energy levels are.

I'm just eating very light food now and not very much compared with what I was eating! I'm drinking whenever I want to though.

Monday 29th November

I have been feeling uneasy about things. I'm not keen to do the twenty one day process at all. I've been wavering on and off about the whole thing in general. Do I really need to do this?

I had the idea of looking on Jasmuheen's website. The book I have been reading about her was written during the nineteen nineties. How does she feel about things now?

Wow!

On the website it confirms everything I have been thinking. Gosh! She has changed! All the things I have been intuitively doing are now in her eyes the correct things to do. She no longer talks about the twenty one day process. She talks about doing this thing gradually! Nearly everything she says on her website confirms my intuitive thoughts. It's like a huge weight of my mind.

Right! I will stay with this process and see where it leads me. I can see now that by continually asking source to be 'clearer' the only road that I *could* take is this one! There's not a lot else major to clear! But what I have been filling my body with, although its not outwardly harming me, is holding up my spiritual progress.

So...............I pray now that I take this process at the right pace and the right way for my own highest good. All will be well.

Wednesday 8th December

The last few days I have been rebelling against the whole idea of 'not eating'. I have been asking for help.

I haven't felt too good in my tummy because of putting some heavier foods in it so yesterday I ate salad and I felt much better. So I woke this morning feeling in good balance and that all was right with the world again. I had to take my car into the garage for a service and as I drove onto the forecourt I hit a post that was frozen into the ground. I hit it gently, I was driving very slowly and I damaged the middle section of one side of my car. I will have to have a new door and a new side panel.

"Why" I asked myself, "why would I do that, when I feel so in balance?"

It didn't take me long to realize that the universe had found a clever way of showing me the damage that I am doing to myself when I eat. I'm damaging my tummy section, gently, nothing serious and there is no one else involved. But the degree of damage to my car is proportionate to the damage I am doing to my tummy. I thought about my car. Wow! It needed a new door and a new side panel. It was exterior work and nothing serious, but expensive to put right and *more damage than I could possibly have believed for such a small incident.* So, I must be doing more damage to my own vehicle (my body) than I had realized, by eating!

Well. I asked for help and I've got it. I will remember the damage to my car for a long while because it is so costly, so I will not forget the unnecessary damage I am doing to my body now.

I've had another thought. As I *know* that I do not need food now, is the damage done by eating increased now? In other words, food didn't damage me in the past because I didn't know I shouldn't eat it but now I know food is superfluous, is it more damaging?

Possibly.

Right! I'd better get my car fixed and I'd better fix myself too.

Thursday 9th December

New regime has started. I don't drink hot chocolate any more and I am tuning in to the foods that I am eating carefully to see if they feel right and I am eating slightly less than I was during the two meals that I do have. I've cut out a lot of hot Ribena drinks and I am having hot water instead.

I feel quite hungry tonight but I know its only habit. Food is *such* a habit.

My energy is the same as usual. Not more not less. My weight feels stable.

Sunday 12th December

I have been feeling hungry so I decided to eat a little more. I'm back to two proper meals a day. I feel tired and I have a cold so that could be throwing things a bit. I think

I will stabilize like this for a few days and then see how I'm led.

Thursday 16th December,

I am so confused. I'm still basically sticking to two meals a day but feeling I should give up meat as it doesn't do me much good. Well it's ok, but I feel I am eating animals' energy and this is affecting my own purity. I think I might go back to going through the twenty one day process after all. I might do it very soon in the New Year but get Christmas over first. Not sure.

Saturday 18th December,

This morning I have shocking news. I have a cyst on my back which has gradually been getting bigger and sorer during the last week. This morning I tried tuning in again to see if I could understand why it is there. What *is* it that I *will not* face? I have been trying so desperately to know, all week.

Suddenly I saw maggots and worm like creatures spilling out of the cyst. To say I was shocked is an understatement. I was devastated. My cyst was showing me that I had been a maggoty wormlike creature that had been one of the first parts of the 'light' to eat! I had been one of the creatures trying to make the journey from one tree to another (so to speak) and I had been one of the first to absorb others!

The guilt I felt at that moment was astronomic. I knew it was true. I recognized that energy within myself. I knew I had been a pioneer at that time, at the forefront of the light forcing outwards from source. I could feel the competitiveness within myself, wanting to be one of the first to make the journey. So I had listened to the call from my fellow beings,

"Eat me, absorb me. We will help you survive the journey"

And I 'absorbed'. Yes, I absorbed. In that moment I helped to create a fresh type of dependency. I moved creation further from source towards thinking that we needed to absorb each other to survive.

I lay in bed, sadly taking in my part of responsibility for that moment. It didn't matter to me that millions of others alive today are also responsible. I took on *my* part of the responsibility, in its entirety. I suddenly understood why I was being shown that I could take the path of 'not eating' if I choose. For if I do so, I could rectify the 'me' that had chosen to eat so long ago. I could reverse my personal part of that unnecessary energy and would therefore be bringing that part of the 'light' back to the planet.

Not only would I be helping the planet in this way, I would also be doing it from a place of plenty. I live in a country where food is overflowing, where every type of food is accessible at almost any time of year. My fridge is full of all I could wish for. I can eat whatever I want............if I choose.

But, if I choose to turn away from it, if I choose to proceed with the twenty one day process or if I choose to prove that I can survive without food, I *will* reverse the damage done so long ago and in the highest possible way.

So, now I have a true purpose. Isn't this what I was asking for? Help? And I now have that help. I *will* do it. I *have* to. I need to live a future where I can truly 'be' in a place where I have no food dependency. It doesn't matter what happens afterwards. I just need to 'do' it. I need to put right my bit of the process.

My fight is over!

I also now know that this diary needs to be a part of my new book. It's no good hiding. I've done that before and it almost killed me. So blow. And blow again! I'm going to have to let it be known.

Sunday 26th December

I can't start the twenty one day process yet. I have too many cysts popping up and I have a lump under my arm. It's all quite scary. I rang my mentor today and she said don't start until I am off the antibiotics and well on the mend. I need to try and find out why the cysts don't seem to be disappearing. Also, what is going on under my arm?

Anyway I've taken myself off dairy products because instinctively I feel that they may be contributing to my cysts. It seems as though I am letting toxins out or trying to?

I have tooth ache today too. Something else is brewing.

Friday 31st December

After a perfectly ghastly few days and after much advice from nutritionists and Jasmuheen herself, I have decided that my cysts, and now an abscess behind my tooth, are not getting better because I am trying to detoxify too fast. In purifying my diet so quickly (have been down to only vegetables and rice today) I am pushing my cells into letting too many toxins into the blood stream and my liver can't cope.

So.............it seems that slow and steady is the rule of thumb. I was only panicking because I thought that if I don't do it now I won't have time again this year because of opening the retreat again in April. But what does it matter if I do or don't do it now? The most important thing is that I have the intention and also that I believe, one hundred per cent, that I *can* live off light. What has happened through this though is that I will be eating a much cleaner and more organic diet from now on.

The experts no longer advocate doing the twenty one day process. They say it only has a ten per cent success rate and has proved too shocking for the body. They now advocate listening to the intuition and doing it slowly............ So............. I've gone full circle.

Ok, I am currently on two types of anti–biotic, one from the doctor and one from the dentist and facing a small operation on Tuesday to remove the cyst. I shall get that done first and see what happens after that.

Saturday 1ˢᵗ January 2011

As I went to sleep last night I asked the universe if there was anything further that I needed to understand at this point.

This morning I awoke to 'further understandings'!!

During the Christmas period when I was enduring all the pain, I lost my way somewhat. I forgot that this process is all about 'cleansing' and it became a mad dash for 'clearing the poisons from my body so that I could get out of pain'. This morning, having calmed myself yesterday, I was able to receive the reality of the situation.

Coming off dairy and meat was entirely right. Coming off sugars at this point was not so necessary, as I had at first supposed. Understanding what different foods do to the body has been invaluable. Starting a cleansing process of all the products in my house is very helpful. I remembered that in the autumn I had been asking that my every day internal clearing process should not be so laborious. I had also constantly been asking to clear myself further from unkind thoughts. In fact I had at one point got so cross with myself for thinking (bad) thoughts that I had said out loud,

"No! I won't have this any more. It's not who I want to be. Please, please help me stop this!"

I realize now that the cyst started to grow at this point and it was indeed coinciding with the cut down of snacks which of course meant I was taking in less of the harmful products. My body started to react and my liver started to be overloaded with the toxins trying to escape, so cysts and other eliminations started to appear through my skin.

When I cut out dairy on Boxing Day I must have been overloading my liver again and so the cysts couldn't recover as they were still needed as exit points. My poor body! It's been trying to clear itself of animal energies and I've been fighting the clearing process! So I have now asked the universe to help my liver to cope and to allow the drainage of the toxins to come out in the normal way so that my skin can recover. I am well into the main part of eliminating the toxins, so it should be ok.

I have now understood that I have had to undergo an increasingly laborious 'cleansing of energy' process on a several times a day basis, because I was choosing to ingest animal energies. If I now went back to eating animal energies I would have to do this again, in order to maintain the level of clarity that I have grown used to. If I choose *not* to eat animal energies I will not need to laboriously clear myself from their energies. It's my choice! This will also apply to sugars, vegetables and anything else that I choose to eliminate from my system, at some later stage, should I decide to continue this process and cleanse further. But next time I will understand the process and will do it more calmly, slowly and gently so that my body can cope.

I have noticed that on several occasions in the last few weeks my spontaneous reactions to certain situations have improved and I have been surprised and very pleased. Now I know why.

Of course my choice is that I do not wish to ingest animal energy again. I know that if it happens by accident it doesn't matter at all. I will simply ask to clear my body of the offending energies.

Sunday 2nd January

I am trying not to fight what I *have* to do. My whole self wants to go back to eating and drinking my old diet. I yearn for what I am used to, food that I know, normality. If I had a choice I would eat what I have always eaten and just die when my number is up. This whole process, for me, is torture.

As I lay in the bath I pondered my misery. I fully allowed the emotion to swamp me and then I started to remember countless past lives in which I had died from starvation. I was amazed and yet not amazed. But I now understood my paralyzing fear…………...

Later that day I sat eating my vegetable supper in complete misery. I asked for help. My whole body screamed for help. And of course, help came.

Our whole purpose on this planet is to 'consciously' return to the level of light that exists at source. Our current major step is to bring back the light as it was before the split. The actual moment of rebalancing is approaching fast. I can feel an urgency that is unrelenting. There is no more time to waste. There are humans incarnate now who are working unbelievably hard to bring the rebalance about. I am one of those humans, but there are others doing better than me. If I achieve reaching the level of light that we had before the split I am bringing that level of light *voluntarily* into consciousness. My sacrifice is not just a selfish sacrifice. By living in one of the most affluent countries in the world, where any food I want is at my fingertips, and voluntarily giving the tastiest bits up, I am taking myself back to the level of the light before the split. On a personal level I am making up for my past and on a world level I am enabling the light to come through me at the level the planet needs right now.

Slowly my cyst continues to improve. Slowly the toxins are eliminating themselves. Slowly I will take these last steps as guided and needed……………………..

Thursday 6ᵗʰ January

All is on course. My skin continues to improve. My state of mind is rebalancing. My body is getting used to its new regime. I am healing.……

I will let the future take care of itself!

Sunday 9ᵗʰ January

I cannot describe adequately in words what is going on now. I just know that I am daily becoming an increasingly effective channel for the level of light that existed on earth before the split. Joy, peace, love and wisdom are coming back into balance deep within me.

I have *yearned* for this moment. I have yearned to reconnect with this level of light. I know I have still so much to learn but I have cleared myself enough at this point in time to feel the benefits of all my past efforts and to know they have been worthwhile. I represent in my small way, the truth of all that I have searched for.

Chapter Eight

Into the future.............

I had been considering a visit to Machu Picchu for around a year and I had collated a list of people who intimated that they would like to come with me. However I had no idea of the revelations that were about to come.....................

I awoke one morning in a trancy type of state, with the energy of the split encompassing me. It was a very strong sensation and I became aware that I had been around the Machu Picchu area at the time of the split. I 'saw' a huge volcanic basin and I knew it had just exploded. There had been a large community living there and the eruption caused the community to become engulfed in rocks and lava. All I could see was the crest of the basin and I saw a wonderful dawn coming up from behind the dark crest.

I was told that my journey to Machu Picchu could be very special indeed. By making a personal pilgrimage to the area, the universe could use it to bring back an enormous part of the 'light' that had been lost at that time. I could take consciousness up the mountain and because I had been there at the time of the split, all sorts of growth would come for me as I remember things and at the same time I would be gifting the planet beyond anything I had ever dreamed possible.

I started to think about the people who had shown interest in coming with me. I knew that it was no coincidence that they wanted to accompany me. I knew that they also had lived nearby the explosion at the same time. Our combined energy could serve the planet enormously and I knew that they too could benefit as I would.

It came to me that the timing and the arrangements for the whole expedition would be totally in the hands of the universe. The whole thing was so much bigger than us that all I had to do was to follow my intuition to the letter and it would all go perfectly. That was a terrific relief!

I knew that if we or I chose to do this, we would be bringing an enormous chunk of the 'rebalancing' of our planet to fruition at a very important moment in the planet's history. I saw the sun rise over the crest of the volcano and I saw it as part of the dawning of a new era. This new era would start when the planet achieved enough of a rebalance to allow 'light' to be in the majority once more.

And so we are going to work. Four of us so far are planning to go on this expedition. It will be what it will be. I wonder how many others are preparing for other such missions all over the world............silently, busily, dutifully, selflessly.

IT'S AWESOME.

Afterword

It is important to note that these writings ended on 10th January 2011.

The universe is currently spinning us so fast that what was true on the above date will already have altered. But, I had to stop somewhere. I felt I should try and put these revelations into print as best I could, because they have changed the lives of so many already. In return I would be grateful if you could share/pass on what is written here with those who you feel are ready to receive this.

More copies of 'The Butterfly spreads it's Wings or my first book – 'From Chrysalis to Butterfly' are available from Amazon.co.uk, from the publishers or directly from myself at:- www.cotswoldhealingretreat.com

Be the light.

Spread the light.

Share your light.

We are one.

About the Author

I have been a channel for healing for most of my life. My training has come direct from the source of all that is and has been intense, soul searching and yet very rewarding. I am now learning more about the 'bigger picture' that surrounds us, moving from beyond the history of this planet into understanding what the universe is all about. This learning enhances all that i do to help people and takes me ever closer towards enlightenment.

My sole purpose in life is to 'serve'. I have fun inbetween 'serving' but even whilst having fun I remain true to who I am. The more I grow the happier I am and the more light finds its way through me onto the planet.

I live on a beautiful farm in the Cotswolds which I open as a retreat during the summer months. People from all over the world come and enjoy the seclusion, tranquillity and peace that embraces the farm at all times. The guests receive healing and unconditonal love whilst staying, either from myself, the place itself or other guests. The farm definately catapults those who are 'searching' for their deepest truths into a fast forwarding process which is very beneficial, taking them on their journey with increased speed.

My youngest son currently lives on the farm with me which is a great joy and support. My daughter lives in London and is learning her life lessons in the best place for her. She visits me regularly. We are a very close family and the guests who visit are embraced in this 'family' as equals.

Lightning Source UK Ltd.
Milton Keynes UK
177873UK00002B/41/P

9 781456 775377